GANGS

Lori Hile

Heinemann
LIBRARY

Chicago, Illinois

www.capstonepub.com
Visit our website to find out more information about Heinemann-Raintree books.

To order:
☎ Phone 800-747-4992
🖥 Visit www.capstonepub.com
to browse our catalog and order online.

© 2013 Heinemann Library
an imprint of Capstone Global Library, LLC
Chicago, Illinois

Edited by Andrew Farrow, Adam Miller, and
 Vaarunika Dharmapala
Designed by Steve Mead and Clare Webber

Originated by Capstone Global Library Ltd
Printed and bound in China by Leo Paper Products Ltd

16 15 14 13 12
10 9 8 7 6 5 4 3 2 1

Library of Congress Cataloging-in-Publication Data

Hile, Lori.

 Gangs / Lori Hile.

  p. cm.—(Teen issues)

 Includes bibliographical references and index.

 ISBN 978-1-4329-6535-8 (hb)—ISBN 978-1-4329-6540-2 (pb) 1. Gangs. 2. Violent crimes—Prevention. I. Title.

 HV6437.H55 2013

 364.106'6—dc23   2011039238

Acknowledgments

We would like to thank the following for permission to reproduce photographs: Alamy p. 36 (© Michael Matthews—Police Images); Corbis pp. 7 (© Aristide Economopoulos/Star Ledger), p. 13 (© Jerome Sessini), 14 (© Jay Dickman), 18 (© Keith Dannemiller), 23 (© Ted Soqui), 29 (© Carlos Cazalis), 39 (© Scott Houston), 42 (© Daniel LeClair/Reuters), 48 (© Alex Masi); Courtnewsuk p. 11 (Ed Willcox); Getty Images pp. 24 (CNN), 44 (Scott Strazzante/Chicago Tribune/McClatchy-Tribune), 47 (Clayton Chase); Photolibrary pp. 4 (Francesca Yorke), 20 (Janine Wiedel), 26 (Uwe Umstätter/Mauritius); Shutterstock pp. 17 (© Yaro), 34 (© Helga Esteb), 40 (© James Steidl); Rex Features p. 32 (Steve Burton).

Cover photograph of young people reproduced with permission of Photolibrary (Stockbroker). Cover photograph of broken glass and cracks reproduced with permission of Shutterstock (© Olegusk).

In order to protect the privacy of individuals featured in this book, some names may have been changed.

Every effort has been made to contact copyright holders of any material reproduced in this book. Any omissions will be rectified in subsequent printings if notice is given to the publisher.

CONTENTS

Types of Gangs 4

Life in a Gang.. 14

Why Do Gangs Form? 24

Gangs and the Media....................................32

Police vs. Gangs 36

Getting Out, Staying Out 40

What Have We Learned? 48

Research and Debate 50

Glossary 52

Find Out More.. 54

Index 56

Some words are shown in bold, **like this**. You can find out what they mean by looking in the glossary.

TYPES OF GANGS

People usually join gangs when they are just children or teenagers, before they understand the negative effect gang activity can have on themselves and others.

True stories: Gang murders

- In 2011, on Halloween, five-year-old Aaron Shannon was excited to wear his Spider-Man costume and go trick-or-treating. As he ran around his Los Angeles backyard, showing off his costume, **gang** members appeared in the alley. Believing a member of a rival gang was in Aaron's home, they began to shoot. Aaron died the next day from gunshot injuries to his head. No one in Aaron's family was connected to gangs.

- Jamiel Shaw, 17, a football star at his Los Angeles high school, was walking home when a car pulled up next to him. The driver asked Jamiel what gang he was in, then shot Jamiel before he could answer. Jamiel's father was at home, not far away. He heard the shots and ran outside to find his son dead. The young man convicted of Jamiel's murder was a member of the 18th Street gang. His gang's bitter rivals, the Bloods, held territory near Jamiel's house.

- Pepe Brown, gang leader of the Holly Street Boys, heard that two members of a rival gang had flirted with his girlfriend. He decided to hunt them down. Pepe and his crew arrived at the place in London, England, where the boys had been spotted. The boys were gone, but Pepe shot his gun anyway. Two bullets hit an 18-year-old man named Jadie Brissett. Jadie managed to climb over a wall before he died, next to some garbage cans.

Gangs and tragedy

When gangs make headlines, the stories are usually tragic ones. They are also very similar, often involving teenagers killing children or other teenagers who happened to be in the wrong place at the wrong time, who lived in the "wrong" territory or belonged to the "wrong" gang. The killing is usually senseless. Yet it continues. Why?

People get involved with gangs for many reasons: problems at home, a desire for acceptance, excitement, or money. Most make the decision to join when they are just kids—9, 12, 16 years old. The sooner you learn more about gangs, the easier it will be for you to make good choices and help your friends to do the same.

Gangs by the numbers

Only about 8 percent of young people actually join gangs but, according to estimates, there are about 40,000 different gangs in the United States alone. Some studies show they are responsible for up to 80 percent of crimes across the country. In Los Angeles county, a gang capital, over 15,000 people died from gang-related violence between 1988 and 2008. That is three times the number of U.S. soldiers who died in the Iraq War.

What is a gang?

The desire to be part of a group, whether it is a family or **peers**, is natural. However, street gangs are different from other groups. Gangs often engage in serious criminal activities such as drug dealing, rape, and murder. Gang leaders themselves are often very young. Most gang members range in age from 12 to 24 years, although some can be in their thirties and forties. Most of these older members, sometimes called OGs (original gangsters), have simply aged with the gang and know no other life. The majority of street gangs have an official gang name, sign or symbol, and code of conduct, along with a specified "territory." To defend that territory, gang members will fight and sometimes kill. Gangs also expect lifelong loyalty. Once you join a gang, it can be difficult to get out.

Modern street gangs

Gangs have been around in various forms for many years, but a few things have changed in recent times. Gangs now use the Internet to recruit new members and promote drugs and other services to customers. This allows them to reach a larger group of people and round up members for street battles more quickly.

Gangs are also deadlier now than in the past. Members are more likely to use guns and knives. Many of these guns are high-caliber, **semi-automatic** weapons, which means that the shooters can hit several targets at once, from long distances. This also means that stray bullets often hit innocent **bystanders**. Fortunately, people are more aware of the dangers of gangs these days and are working hard to prevent violence and combat gangs.

This policeman is displaying an AK-47 assault rifle that was used in a gang murder in Newark, New Jersey.

THINK ABOUT THIS

In the video game "Grand Theft Auto," players take on the role of gang members. They earn points for killing rivals and completing "missions" such as thefts and **assassinations**. Many people believe violent video games teach children that robbery and murder are acceptable and exciting. Some studies show that children who spend more time watching violent images behave more aggressively toward others. Other studies show that those who play the most violent video games are already more **antisocial** than other children. Some argue that it is better for people to act out their aggression on computers instead of in the real world. What do you think?

Gangs

There are a number of different types of gangs, including:

- *Commercial gangs*: Some gangs, especially in Chicago, Illinois, and Dublin, Ireland, are like corporations. They focus on making money, often through selling illegal drugs. They have highly organized structures. They try to steer clear of violence, because it scares away customers, but they will fight if another gang threatens their business.

- *Racial and ethnic gangs*: Often certain racial or ethnic groups will band together for acceptance and protection. There are black, Latin American, Jamaican, Vietnamese, and other ethnic gangs. Like the commercial gangs, many ethnic gangs sell drugs or other illegal goods.

- *Social or street gangs*: More common in Los Angeles and London, social or street gangs are looser and less structured than commercial gangs. They are groups of young people who hang out together because they share common problems and circumstances. Many of these gangs engage in random violence and have only casual, unwritten rules.

- *Suburban and rural gangs*: Since police in big cities have created sophisticated units to crack down on gangs, many big city gangsters are moving their members to suburbs, where the police do not know them. Suburbs also have gangs of their own. These include delinquent gangs, who engage in occasional violence and theft, as well as drinking and drug use.

  Gangs have also spread far from cities into small-town, rural parts of the United States like Minnesota and Utah. This rise in gangs is in part because city gangs have spread out their network of drug dealing. In some cases, it is because young people are bored or looking for a release from the economic hardships that have hit some farming communities.

- *Hate gangs*: Hate gangs are formed by people who share beliefs about certain racial or ethnic groups. For example, many members of **skinhead** gangs believe that white people are superior to other races. They often direct violence against Jewish and black people.

A day in the life of a gang member

Younger gang members often serve as foot soldiers for older members. They spend a lot of time waiting for orders. In between actions, they may use drugs and alcohol, share war stories, or go to gang parties. They may get bored and take part in unplanned crimes, such as car theft or vandalism. These crimes attract the attention of the police, which helps distract them from the more organized crimes of older members.

In drug gangs, members may spend days selling drugs and recruiting new customers by handing out business cards or free drug samples. Some samples are stronger than the usual supply, in order to attract new business. Users may die of overdoses.

Gang members also spend time settling scores. They may attack rivals for small offenses, such as spilling a drink or talking with a member's girlfriend. Other gang activities may include robbing stores or houses, selling stolen goods, and producing fake documents, such as passports.

Youth gangs around the world

UNITED KINGDOM:
London Fields Boys, Holly Street Boys, Burger Bar Boys, Pepperhill Mob, Croxteth Crew, Sheffield Gang, Nogga Dogs

UNITED STATES AND CANADA:
Crips, Bloods, Gangster Disciple Nation, Black Gangsters, Latin Kings, Black P. Stone Nation, Vice Lords, 18th Street Gang, MS-13

SPAIN:
Latin Kings, Netas, MS-13

MEXICO:
Los Zetas, MS-13

KENYA:
Mungiki (Kenyan Mafia)

AUSTRALIA:
Bra Boys, EDT

CENTRAL AMERICA:
MS-13

BRAZIL:
Primeiro Comando da Capital

This map shows you where some of the world's most **notorious** youth gangs are located.

Girl gangs

In December 2004, a 68-year-old woman living in Washington, D.C., received a threatening phone call. Some gang members told her, "We're going to put you in a coma." It was not young men who made the call. It was young women. They were girl gang members, at "war" with another girl gang—one that the woman's granddaughter belonged to.

Over the past 20 years, more girls have joined gangs or taken on new roles within their gangs. In the past, girls mainly provided support or affection for their gang boyfriends or helped them smuggle or stow weapons and drugs. More recently, girls have become equal partners with boys, performing all the same activities. The only difference is their gang names. They sometimes call themselves "Latin Queens" instead of Latin Kings, or "Lady Disciplettes" rather than the Gangster Disciples.

Reasons for girl gang growth

The rise in girl gangsters can be tied partly to harsher police crackdowns. For example, in 2002, Los Angeles enacted a "three strike" policy, in which offenders convicted of three violent crimes were automatically sentenced to at least 25 years in prison. Soon, prisons were overcrowded with men, leaving women to fill in for them on the streets.

Some girl gang members also felt disrespected by the boys in their gangs. Even though the girls put in the same amount of work or even did more work, they were treated as second-class citizens by the boys. Boys sometimes prevented girls from being leaders and expected girls to perform sexual favors. Some girls grew tired of this treatment and formed their own, all-girl gangs: no boys allowed!

Girl gangs give girls more power and independence, but they also bring more dangers. In the past, some boys tried to protect the girls in their neighborhoods. Now, they may kill or be killed by girls.

Girl gangsters by the numbers

Of an estimated one million gang members in the United States, about 80,000 are female, ranging in age from 9 to 24. An estimated 20 percent of New York City gang members are girls.

Paying the price

But being in a gang leads to serious consequences for anyone. Girl gangsters, just like boys, are paying the price for their crimes. In the United States, the number of women in prison has tripled since the late 1980s.

CHELSEA BENNET: A FATAL STABBING

In June 2007, police were called to an apartment in Croydon, in South London. Seventeen-year-old Sian Simpson had been stabbed in the heart and killed by a girl gang member, Chelsea Bennett, 19. When the police arrived, they found a large group of girls at the scene, kicking, screaming, and throwing bricks at Bennett's car windows. Bennett survived this attack.

The fight centered on jealousies over a man who had fathered children with two of the girls at the scene. Girl gang members often have disputes over relationships, just like non-gang girls. Unfortunately, the addition of guns or knives can cause these confrontations to turn deadly.

Chelsea Bennet used a 10-inch (25-centimeter) blade to stab Sian Simpson.

Not one of the boys

Female gang members can be just as brutal as boys, but they often operate differently:

- *They rely more on weapons*: Girls, on average, are less muscular than boys, so they often rely on weapons, rather than their fists, in fights. They tend to use knives and razor blades and strike at people's faces. Women also use guns more frequently than men, which may be one reason their attacks often become deadly faster.

- *It's personal*: Unlike men, women rarely attack random strangers. Instead, they are more likely to target someone who has hurt or threatened them, a family member, or their partner. This can make women's battles more personal, intense, and deadly.

- *They blend in better*: Girls in gangs often have part-time jobs, which gives them a professional appearance and also allows them to engage more easily in **white-collar crimes**, such as identity theft, computer-chip theft, and **card cloning**. Girl gang members may sometimes have babies, which also makes them appear less suspicious.

- *They mature faster*: Many girls grow out of gangs sooner than boys. A Canadian police murder investigator says, "Most violent girls don't stay violent. When an 11-year-old boy kills someone in a horrible way, there's usually no hope for him. With girls, it's different. Once girls decide to change, they usually change completely." Often, girls will ultimately value relationships more than power.

- *They use sex as a weapon*: Girls sometimes flirt with boys to lure, trap, or spy on rival gang members. However, if the boys find out they have been fooled, there will be payback.

TRUE OR FALSE?

Gangs are like a family. Members always have your back.

False. In fact, gang members who are caught by the police often "snitch" in exchange for a reduced punishment. When a 14-year-old girl and a 25-year-old man were murdered by seven members of the 204th Street gang in Los Angeles in 2006, only three of them were caught. One gang member told the police the names of the other four members, in exchange for a shorter prison sentence.

Profile of a girl gangster

It is less common for girls to join gangs, but those who do tend to come from even more troubled homes than the boys. Their self-esteem also tends to be lower. One study shows that over 52 percent of girls who join gangs have been **sexually assaulted**, compared to 22 percent of non-gang girls. About 66 percent of that **abuse** is by family members. Girls often see gangs as a way to escape abuse and join a new family. Unfortunately, some of them have come to consider abuse as normal behavior. Many will do anything to be accepted by the gang, even if it includes abuse or unsafe sex. Many gang girls become pregnant or infected with sexually transmitted diseases as early as at the age of 13.

These two girls and their male friend are gang members from San Salvador, El Salvador.

LIFE IN A GANG

Gang initiation ceremonies
can be very violent.

Initiation

Paco watched as the gang members formed two parallel lines, nine members on each side. In just three minutes, he would be a full gang member—if he could walk between the two lines while the gang members kicked, punched, and pummeled him. Paco crossed his arms over his face to protect himself, but fists, feet, and belt buckles still struck his chest and legs, leaving bruises and cuts. His legs wobbled, but he steadied himself. If he fell, he would have to begin again. When he finally staggered to the end, the punches turned to pats on the back. He was now a Black Diamond.

This scene is typical of a gang **initiation rite**, sometimes called a **Violation-in (V-in)** ceremony. Some gang members cannot walk for a week after their initiation. The purpose of the ceremony is for potential members to prove that they are physically and mentally strong enough to fight for the gang and defend it from rivals. It also introduces new members to a gang's violent way of life and gives them a taste of what awaits them, should they break any rules or try to leave the gang.

Other ways to join

The "V-in" is probably the most common initiation rite, but there are other ways to join a gang. Potential members may choose to complete a "mission," which could involve an armed robbery, drive-by shooting, or a stabbing in rival territory. Some lucky members are "blessed in," meaning they can skip initiation rites because they have already proved themselves or had a family member in the gang vouch for them.

Some young women can choose to be "**sexted-in**," rather than beaten-in, which means she has to engage in sexual activity with gang members. Girls who opt for this initiation method tend to receive less respect than the other girls and are rarely considered equal members.

TRUE OR FALSE?

Getting respect is the most important thing in life. If someone insults or disrespects you, you must fight or harm that person.

False. Being shown respect is not the same thing as being feared. Being tough might make people afraid of you, but it will not make them like or respect you. Being respectful of others is a good way to be respected by them.

Codes of conduct

Gang members routinely break society's laws, but most gangs have their own strict codes of conduct that members must memorize and obey. A member of the Texas Syndicate gang revealed his gang's constitution, including the seven rules below. Most gangs have similar requirements:

1. Once a member, always a member.
2. The Texas Syndicate comes before anyone and anything.
3. Right or wrong, the Texas Syndicate is right at all times.
4. All members will get the Texas Syndicate tattoo.
5. Never let a member down.
6. All members will respect each other.
7. Keep all gang information within the group.

Some gangs also forbid members to talk with the media, and almost all gangs share one rule in common: even if a gangster sees another member commit a crime, he or she must never "snitch"—that is, they must never report the activity to the police.

Recently, however, police officers and older gang members are reporting that many younger gang members are more interested in making money than being loyal to their gang and its rules. For example, a young gang member might sell drugs on an unauthorized street, in order to pocket additional money.

Members who are caught breaking gang rules are publicly punished during weekly gang meetings. For instance, after one new female member of the Latin Kings was found having a friendly conversation with a rival gangster, she received a three-minute beating. Although this punishment may seem harsh for merely talking to a rival, gang leaders strive to teach gang members that all rivals are "enemies."

Dress code

Image is very important to gang members, and they gain more respect from their peers if they wear impressive clothes. However, the gangster look has evolved.

For years, many gang members wore baggy trousers, sports jerseys, flashy jewelry, and bandannas. Hardcore members eventually realized that these stereotypical outfits made them more visible to the police.

Today, some gang members wear suits or jeans and white T-shirts, so they can blend in better. They save the more flashy outfits for gang parties. This new style, called "low pro," short for "low profile," makes it more difficult for the police to identify gang members. It also makes it easier for members to commit white-collar crimes, such as identity theft and credit card fraud.

The old gangster look is now more popular with non-gang teenagers than with actual gangsters. This can result in tragic cases of mistaken identity. In 2005, a teenager named Javier Hernandez was shot dead while washing his car near Culver City, California. Gang members saw his baggy shorts, tattoos, and shaved head and wrongly assumed he was a member of a rival gang.

This new look also fools average citizens. Someone might deliberately avoid a group of teenagers wearing stereotypical gang clothes but stand right next to a young man in a suit. This nicely dressed man might suddenly pull out a weapon and demand the person's car keys.

Many gang members are now starting to dress in stylish suits such as the one this model is wearing.

Gang identity

The title of the movie *Colors* (1988) refers to the colors that two rival Los Angeles gangs wear to identify themselves: red for the Bloods, and blue for the Crips. Most gangs have their own colors, but in recent years, U.S. gangs have been concealing them to escape police scrutiny. Many British gangs have only recently adopted U.S.-style gang colors and names. For example, some entire boroughs in London identify with certain colors.

Tragically, ordinary citizens wearing the wrong color in the wrong place can be targeted. In California, 24-year-old Roger Weinert was not in a gang, but he was shot while walking to the house of a family friend. The gang member who shot him assumed he was a rival because of the red jacket he was wearing.

Many gang members have tattoos recording their gang history. They may include the names of friends who have been killed and the number of enemies they themselves have killed.

Almost all gang members have tattoos. This permanent mark is a way for members to display their lifelong loyalty to their gang. All members of the Latin Kings, for example, are required to have a tattoo of their gang symbol (a crown) or the initials "LK." However, gang members are beginning to hide their tattoos. These days, they might have one placed under a shirt, rather than on their face or lower arm.

Communication

To keep their plans secret, most gangs have developed an extensive set of hand signs that allow them to silently communicate when coordinating battles and other events. In the MS-13 gang, lifting up a shirt means "let's go into battle." However, this means that ordinary citizens who gesture in the wrong way in the wrong neighborhood can get into trouble. At a Florida bar, five deaf patrons using sign language were stabbed by a gang member, when he became convinced they were making the hand signs of a rival gang.

Teenagers in gangs often speak in code in front of non-gangsters, as a way to maintain secrecy. For example, some gang members use the code words "birthday boy" to describe a person about to be robbed.

Technology

Most gang members carry at least one cell phone to arrange drug deals and to call or text for back-up during conflicts. But cell phones can also get gang members into trouble. The Federal Bureau of Investigation (FBI) arrested the highest-ranking member of the Latin Kings for **drug trafficking** and conspiracy, based on evidence from cell phone calls he made in prison.

Many gangs also use profiles or videos on YouTube and MySpace to promote their gang, recruit members, and issue threats to rival gangs. Members use privacy settings to prevent the police from accessing their pages.

There are certain areas claimed by gangs as turf. Enemies seen nearby can be shot or stabbed.

Defending turf

Gangs stake out territories based on where the majority of their members live. Territories can include schools, liquor stores, parks, and clubs. Gang members usually interact within their own areas. This limits their freedom to see and experience other parts of a city. One author researching the Los Angeles Bloods and Crips gangs discovered that most members had never even seen the Pacific Ocean, less than 10 miles (16 kilometers) away.

For some gangs, losing territory means losing money, since this is where drug deals are made. Even gangs that do not deal drugs often collect taxes from dealers who do. So, if a drug dealer makes $1,000 in a day, the gang may collect $500 for allowing the dealer to sell on its territory.

Marking boundaries: Graffiti

Gangs often mark the territories they control or want to control with **graffiti**. They spray-paint gang symbols or names of gang members on to walls and other surfaces. Once a territory is claimed by a gang, rivals may try to invade it or reclaim it for themselves. Gang graffiti in the United States has decreased in recent years, as gangs try to escape the watchful eye of the police. However, it is becoming more common in other parts of the world, such as Europe and Central America.

Some gangs also use graffiti to honor members who have died in street battles. For instance, the MS-13 gang will paint giant murals of illegal graffiti in remembrance of dead "soldiers." One gang member says, "Even though the mural will be covered one day, we won't forget him."

Weapons

How do gangs defend their territories? Sometimes they simply beat up rival gang members. More frequently, they use weapons.

In the United States, guns are often purchased legally by citizens with "clean" records, then sold or given to gang members in exchange for drugs or money. Some U.S. gang members are even joining the U.S. military as a way to steal military weapons, ammunition (bullets), and equipment, such as body armor. These members also share the "urban warfare" techniques they learn in the military with their gangs.

Tagger gangs

Almost all gangs create graffiti, but not all graffiti is created by gangs. Some young street artists create graffiti as a form of self-expression, rather than as a way to mark territory. Unlike gang graffiti, which may be crude and basic, graffiti art is often elaborate and intricate. These artists take pride in their art and even take pictures of it before it is removed.

Street artists can anger gangs when they paint over gang graffiti. For that reason, graffiti artists sometimes band together to form tagger gangs. Unlike street gangs, their only crime is creating illegal graffiti. However, they may sometimes carry weapons to protect themselves from street gangs.

The effect of gangs

Gangs can have a huge impact on communities, families, and the members themselves. Simply walking to school through rival gang territory can be risky, and some parents keep their children at home for this reason. In Chicago, many school buses are claimed by particular gangs, making them dangerous for non-members or rival members to catch. One mother used to arm her daughter with weapons such as knives and bats, to protect herself along the way.

In Los Angeles, a young woman was celebrating her high school graduation with a party at her house, located on the boundary between two rival gangs. Suddenly, someone announced the name of the rival gang, then started shooting. One person died and nine were critically injured. None of them was a gang member.

Most hardcore gang members end up either dead or in prison. In the United States, 90 percent of male gang members are arrested at least once by age 18. And 60 percent of male gang members are in prison or dead by age 20. Those who manage to escape gangs often have little or no education, since over 95 percent of male gang members do not finish high school. This leaves them with few job skills or prospects. Gang members are also more likely to be addicted to drugs or alcohol than non-members.

Death as a way of life

Rival gangs often target relatives of gang members as retaliation for crimes. In one inner-city Los Angeles elementary school class, 75 percent of students personally knew someone—a brother, sister, uncle, father, friend—who had been murdered. For many in gang communities, death is a way of life. A Crips member, Young Guess, says, "I'm kind of a professional mourner now." Ana, a member of the Gangster Disciples, says, "You go out, maybe you get shot at. Otherwise, you have to just stay inside your house."

One shocking survey has studied children living in South Central Los Angeles, an area with a high level of gang violence. The survey found that these children have greater levels of **post-traumatic stress disorder (PTSD)**, a severe type of stress sometimes experienced by soldiers at war, than children of similar ages living in war-torn Baghdad, Iraq.

Licensed to kill

Sometimes young gang members do the killing. Alex Cisernos, a former member of the MS-13 gang, is in prison for the murder of a friend-turned-informant. He says, "Gangs can distort reality. Once you join, you lose all respect for life. Your mind closes off from the rest of the world, and you're capable of doing anything for the gang." Like soldiers of war, killing becomes a way of life for some. Even so, many gang members have later expressed horror and great regret for all the pain and suffering they have caused. Many were motivated by this realization to change their ways.

This is the funeral of Stanley "Tookie" Williams, a member of the Crips gang in South Central Los Angeles. The political activist Reverend Jesse Jackson is speaking at the funeral, which was attended by about 2,000 people, including many gang members.

WHY DO GANGS FORM?

In March 1991, four police officers violently beat an African American man named Rodney King, who had been speeding in his car. His beating was caught on camera, and the footage was shown around the world. The officers were cleared of assault, sparking the 1992 Los Angeles riots, which began as a protest at what many saw as outright racism.

BIRD'S STORY: SLAUSON

In the 1960s, a boy known as "Bird" lived with his middle-class family in Los Angeles. When his parents tried to enroll him in the local Boy Scouts group, the troupe leader said that the other parents might object to having an African American boy in the group. After being rejected from several other clubs in the area, Bird and his friends formed their own all-black "street fraternity." They called it Slauson.

Slauson started innocently enough: just a group of friends hanging out. It gave them an identity and a sense of acceptance. It also gave them some power. As individuals, many African Americans felt ignored or shunned by white society. Together, they had a voice.

Soon other areas formed their own groups, and friendly rivalries broke out, then fights. After members of the clubs started selling drugs, more violence erupted. Bird's street club became the basis for the notorious Los Angeles gang the Crips. Another club, the Bloods, became their archrivals.

For all the differences among gangs, the majority of them spring from similar social conditions, including racism, ethnic discrimination, poverty, poor schools, unemployment, and broken homes. People living in these conditions often feel isolated from the rest of society. They may feel driven to create a society of their own, complete with their own rules.

Racial discrimination

In Los Angeles in the 1940s, many white home owners were legally restricted from selling their homes to black people. Even wealthy African American families were kept out of upper-middle-class suburbs. This forced African American communities to cluster together in poorer areas, on the edges of the city. Those who wandered too far from these areas report being stopped by the police. Some were questioned or beaten. Racial minorities all over the world face similar problems, and many of them form gangs for power, protection, and a sense of identity.

ALEX'S STORY: MS-13

Alex Sanchez fled El Salvador in 1979, to escape a civil war. However, he soon found himself "terrorized" by Mexican and African American street gangs in Los Angeles. Alex and a group of his friends formed a gang of their own for protection. He said, "It started as a bunch of kids ... into heavy metal music. Our biggest worry was not getting tickets for the Ozzy Osbourne concert." Eventually, the group became the basis for MS-13, one of the world's most dangerous gangs.

Conditions that produce gangs

Many newly arrived immigrants face threats and harassment from more established minority groups or from members of the majority community in their new country. They often band together to protect themselves.

Some street gangs do not last long; others stick around for generations. Why do some gangs fade out, while others remain? The biggest factor is not race or ethnicity, but rather the level of wealth and job opportunities within the community. If jobs and other opportunities are available, gangs usually disappear. If there is limited access to good schools and good jobs, gangs stick around.

Young people in gang communities often have lots of unsupervised free time to "hang out" on the streets. Their communities may offer few organized activities, and many parents cannot afford after-school classes or activities.

Poor schools

Schools in communities where gangs tend to form often lack basic educational resources such as computers. They may have difficulty attracting good teachers, which reduces the quality of education offered to students, as well as their chances of going on to college. However, even the best teachers face huge obstacles. Many students have inherited a negative attitude toward school from their parents, who may have dropped out of school themselves. Many students have never been exposed to successful role models who have benefited from education. Instead, they see gang members all around them, who seem to make money with little or no schooling.

Some students do not feel safe walking through their school hallways. Young people cannot focus on schoolwork if they are worried about survival or if they are distracted by a stressful family life. Pregnancy and poverty also prevent young people from attending or focusing on school. Teachers often have little understanding of what their students experience outside the classroom and therefore have little chance of reaching them inside. As a result, communities with gangs have much higher rates of high school dropouts than other communities.

TRUE OR FALSE?

Gangs protect their communities.

False. Gangs often brag that they provide protection for community members by defending them from rival gangs. In reality, citizens are much safer in communities without any gangs at all. Gang members themselves face constant threats from rival gangs, who try to invade territories or retaliate for crimes. About half the victims of gang violence simply happen to be in the wrong place at the wrong time. Gang members are also more likely to be shot by their own members than by rivals because of accidents or disagreements between members.

Profile of a gang member

Not everyone who grows up in a community with gang activity becomes a member. Why are some people more likely to join than others? Many gang members share similar backgrounds.

REYMUNDO'S STORY: FAMILY ABUSE

Reymundo began life in Puerto Rico. His father often beat his mother, before abandoning the family. His mother remarried and moved the family to the United States. There, Reymundo struggled in school, because he did not understand the language. Reymundo's stepfather abused his mother, and they both frequently beat Reymundo with a baseball bat and whipped him with electrical cords. Once, Reymundo's stepfather aimed a gun directly at Reymundo's head and cocked the weapon. Reymundo says he survived this only because his mother and sisters jumped in front of him. Then his mother slapped Reymundo in the face and swore at him. In the end, Reymundo joined the Latin Kings gang as a way to escape his own family.

As horrible as Reymundo's background is, many young people who join gangs face similar kinds of issues. In one study of suburban and urban gangs, every member suffered from at least one of the following problems: **domestic abuse**, child abuse, parents with severe problems such as drug addiction or mental illness, or an absent parent. In fact, 60 percent of gang members experienced three or more of these problems, and 44 percent reported all four.

Many teenagers who join gangs feel there is no one in their life they can trust. Having even one supportive parent or mentor means a teenager is less likely to join a gang. However, some people are simply "born into gangs." If their parents are gang members, they may see no alternative.

Many people who join gangs come from areas, such as this slum in Tijuana, Mexico, with high unemployment, high rates of drug and alcohol abuse, and many other serious social problems.

THINK ABOUT THIS

People often say they join gangs to gain respect. However, respect is sometimes confused with fear. Joining a gang may make people fear you, but it will not make people respect you.

Respect means having a deep admiration for someone, and it must be earned. This requires effort, just like earning money or good grades, but when you believe in yourself, you will not need to gain approval from anyone else. Here are some tips:

- *Be true to yourself*: People respect those who are not afraid to be themselves. Do what you think is right, even if it is not popular.

- *Be cool*: Returning insults or punches will only make you a target. It makes sense to just move on.

- *Study*: One former gang member remembers making fun of a "geek" in high school. Now that "geek" is a doctor, and the gang member is in prison. Who do you think gets more respect?

CASE STUDY: PRAN'S STORY

Pran's parents fled war-torn Cambodia for the United States before he was born. While his father worked long hours and his mother was busy raising his younger brothers and sisters, Pran watched the gangsters in the nearby park. They always wore cool clothes, drove fancy cars, and attracted lots of girls. When he got older, Pran began hanging out with them. Just six months later, he was arrested for selling heroin and sent to prison for four years.

The appeal of gangs

Pran joined a gang for a lot of the same reasons most teenagers do. Here is a closer look at some of the reasons young people join gangs, as well as the realities of gang life:

Reason	Reality
Sense of belonging/acceptance	
Teenagers from troubled families may turn to gangs for the love, loyalty, and acceptance that young people crave and their own families cannot provide.	Almost every gang member who has been to prison reports that it was their blood family, not members of their gang, who came to visit.
Need for protection	
Young people have a need and right to feel safe. In rough areas, many turn to gangs because there is safety in numbers.	The life expectancy of gang members is much lower than it is for non-gang members.
Peer pressure	
Sometimes gangs lure teenagers by offering them free drugs or alcohol. More often, however, teenagers simply join because they see their friends doing it and they do not want to feel left out.	In the end, people in gangs are the ones who get left behind. Most will not finish their education, and many will end up in prison or dead.

Reason	Reality
Money	
For teenagers with nothing, the promise of fast money and status can be hard to resist.	Very few gangsters make big money. Gang members who do have lots of money, drugs, or possessions live in constant fear of being attacked, robbed, or sent to prison.
Drugs	
Many teenagers grow up in families where drug use is common, and they join gangs to gain access to drugs.	Many gang members become addicted to drugs and commit crimes that they would not otherwise commit.
Getting girlfriends/boyfriends	
One self-described geek avoided gangs until he noticed that gang members were surrounded by girls.	Many gangsters have never had healthy role models for relationships, and they often end up abusing their partners.
Only life they know	
To many teenagers, gangs are just part of their community. What might seem threatening to an outsider seems normal to these young people.	Gang life is not normal or acceptable. Gang members break laws and endanger lives. There are many more productive, legitimate lifestyles.
Bad treatment by police	
Some young people report being humiliated by police just for hanging out. One gang member says, "I decided if these guys are going to mistreat me because they think I'm a gang member, I might as well be one."	If a police officer assumes you belong to a gang, why prove them right? While a few officers are corrupt, most work hard to protect citizens.
The thrill	
Some teenagers are simply bored. Gangs provide action and excitement, as well as a distraction from the problems they may be suffering from at home.	Gangs simply create new, even bigger problems.

GANGS AND THE MEDIA

The 2011 riots in London and other cities in England were blamed on gangs. However, many people dispute this, saying there is no evidence that gang members played a leading part in the disturbances.

In August 2011, violence erupted on city streets throughout England after police shot and killed 29-year-old Mark Duggan. People threw gasoline bombs at the police, set patrol cars on fire, looted stores, and burned buses.

UK Prime Minister David Cameron blamed much of the rioting on youth gangs and declared an "all-out war on gangs and gang culture." News articles and television reports soon focused heavily on England's "gang problem." However, some former gang members and scholars believe these media depictions were over-simplified and unfair. While some of the rioters were gang members, there is little evidence to suggest that the majority of the rioting was an organized gang activity. Some of the rioters were simply young people (and even well-off older people) who got caught up in the drama.

The media may present a distorted view of gangs because the public responds to having a clear villain to blame for a crisis. Reporting on gang activity also makes for exciting news coverage, which boosts ratings. Unfortunately, this exaggerated focus on gangs can make gangs themselves seem exciting. It can also create fear among ordinary people, which is exactly what gangs want. Gangs aim to scare and **intimidate** people. They will be equally happy to let the media do it for them.

The media spotlight

Gang members enjoy the media spotlight because it gives them the attention they crave—even if it is negative—and helps them establish a reputation for themselves within their gangs. However, gangs get scared when the media start revealing their secrets.

Irish journalist Veronica Guerin made it her mission to investigate an Irish drug gang in Dublin, Ireland. At first, the gang enjoyed appearing in the newspaper. When she started digging deeper into their world, however, she began to receive threats. One day, as she was driving, gangsters in a car pulled up next to her and shot her in the head. She died instantly.

Gangsta rap

Some people worry that the depictions of gangs in the entertainment media glorify gang life or make it look cooler than it is. They fear this may encourage young people to join gangs, or at least imitate their behavior.

In the 1988 album *Straight Outta Compton*, rap group NWA describe young men going on a warpath that will result in a "bloodbath of cops, dyin' in LA." In 2009, rapper Eminem released a song called "Stay Wide Awake," with lyrics about brutally assaulting a woman in a park. Both of these songs are forms of **gangsta rap**, a type of **hip-hop** music with lyrics that focus on inner-city gang life. Gangsta rap is often **controversial**, because many people believe the explicit lyrics promote rage against the police, hatred of women and gay people, murder, other antisocial behavior, and **materialism**. They worry that young people who listen to gangsta rap may start to believe that violence and criminal activity are normal or even acceptable.

Curtis Jackson, also known as 50 Cent, left his violent gang lifestyle behind and became a successful rap artist.

"It looked so easy in the movies, and we thought we could get away with it, too."

A Chicago gang member, when asked why he committed crimes

However, defenders of gangsta rap point out that rappers have the right to free speech, or the right to say what they want, and that gangsta rappers are actually positive role models for young people. Despite growing up in poor neighborhoods, these artists have carved out legitimate, successful lives for themselves. For example, 50 Cent was inspired to become a rapper after hearing how rapper Notorious B.I.G. pulled himself out of a violent gang lifestyle through music.

THINK ABOUT THIS

The movie *Scarface* (1932) shows gangsters using machine guns to massacre seven members of a rival gang. It horrified many people, who worried that *Scarface*, like many other popular gangster movies of the era, made the lives of gangsters look thrilling. After some off-screen scandals around the same time, Hollywood decided to clean up its image. So, from 1934 to 1968, Hollywood adopted the Hays Code. Under the code, all filmmakers had to keep their movies "family-friendly." For example, they had to make sure that criminals did not seem glamorous. Gangsters in movies were then always caught and harshly punished for their crimes.

When the Hays Code was replaced by a new ratings system in 1968, movies became more explicit in their depictions of violence. The movie *Colors* (1988), which showed a feud between the Bloods and the Crips, introduced a detailed picture of gang culture to people who had never seen it before. According to some accounts, membership in the Crips increased in certain cities after the movie's release.

This raises some questions. Can movies about gangs really influence teenagers to join? What is more important: freedom of expression, or trying to discourage gang membership? Some argue that young people need morals to be clearly shown in movies, but others say that a movie alone will not cause someone to commit violent acts.

POLICE VS. GANGS

Plain-clothes police officers are searching these suspects in New York City. Some people who live in gang communities believe they are unfairly targeted by the police.

Many gang members proudly display their colors and tattoos and openly hang out in public places. Why don't the police simply arrest them and shut the gangs down?

For one thing, it is not illegal to be in a gang. To arrest someone, the police must have evidence of illegal activity, which can be difficult to produce. Second, victims and witnesses of gang crime often fail to report the activity to the police, out of fear of gang intimidation and retaliation.

After one Chicago couple reported a gang shooting that took place outside their house, they were targeted for years by gang members. In this way, gangs train members of their community to see them, and not the police, as their primary form of protection. As one gang member put it, "They can deal with the police or deal with us—and they've got to see us every day."

Distrust and fear

Many communities plagued by gang activity distrust the police as much as they distrust the gangs. The police are sometimes slower to respond to emergency calls in these areas than in wealthier ones. Some gang members have reported waiting three hours or more for the police to arrive after a shootout in their areas.

Some people face discrimination from police officers. They report being called racist names or even beaten. Some have also witnessed examples of police corruption. For instance, officers have raided gang parties and taken drug money for themselves. In Honduras, some police officers have even engaged in drug trafficking. Police there have given weapons and money to gangs to kill rival gang members. This way, the police do not have to enter the dangerous gang territories themselves.

Attacks on the police

Police officers are often right to be afraid of gangs. In the United States, the number of attacks on police officers continues to rise. In many cities, gang members simply outnumber police. In Chicago, for instance, there are about 80,000 gang members and only 13,000 officers. Police believe they need more resources, as well as more streamlined national strategies, to combat gangs.

Mass arrests

At times, police do conduct large-scale gang raids. In February 2012, a unit of London's Metropolitan Police known as the Trident Gang Crime Command arrested over 200 people in raids across the city. They also seized stashes of heroin, cocaine, cannabis, firearms, ammunition, stolen cell phones, and large amounts of cash.

Sometimes raids like these reduce violence and, at least temporarily, weaken gangs. At other times, police have discovered that it does not pay to arrest gang members, since those members will just be replaced by others. Sometimes police prefer to work with known gang leaders, in an attempt to **negotiate** gang **truces** (agreements to stop fighting).

The cycle of violence

Another problem with the mass imprisonment of gang members is that it often continues the cycle of violence. This is how:

- It takes men off the streets. Some of these men are fathers, so this breaks up their families. This can result in teenagers seeking male role models in gangs.
- Someone always fills the hole left by the gang member. In many cases, women fill in for men who are jailed.
- Once prisoners return to society, they often have a hard time finding legitimate jobs. Few employers want to hire ex-prisoners. Furthermore, many criminals do not have job skills. Instead, they often return to doing what they know: committing crimes.
- Prison teaches people to become better criminals. Prisoners spend their time with other criminals, who may teach them new methods for committing crimes. They may also strengthen criminal networks in prison, which helps them conduct crimes once they get out.

Street safety

- Do not wear known gang colors or use any kind of known gang hand signs in public.
- Stay away from strangers in cars who stop to ask you questions.
- Steer clear of known gang hangouts or social events.

Prison gangs

A big problem with the mass imprisonment of gang members is that they often form or join prison gangs, which can be even more dangerous and deadly than street gangs. After all, all the members are convicted criminals, who are violent or ruthless. Many are already serving long sentences, which means they may have nothing to lose.

Many prisoners are killed while in prison. In the state of Texas alone, as many as 54 prisoners were killed by gang violence in just one year.

The influence of prison gangs extends beyond prison walls. Many prison gangs also call the shots for street gangs. In Guatemala, the MS-13 gang planned seven attacks from prison in one year, killing 35 rival gang members on the streets.

Many police have started separating gang members and making them spend 23 hours a day in a prison cell. This reduces prison murders and also the possibility of communicating with the outside world. However, it is also very expensive.

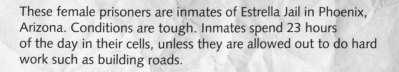

These female prisoners are inmates of Estrella Jail in Phoenix, Arizona. Conditions are tough. Inmates spend 23 hours of the day in their cells, unless they are allowed out to do hard work such as building roads.

GETTING OUT, STAYING OUT

Prison can be a wake-up call for many gang members.

BRENDA'S STORY: MS-13

Brenda Paz started hanging out with MS-13 when she was just 11, and she joined the gang at 13. By the age of 17, she felt bad about what she was doing. She became a "rat" (an informant for the police). She told officers about MS-13's hand signs, weapons, and drug sources. In return, the police gave Brenda money and kept her in a safe place. However, all her friends were gang members, and she started hanging out with them again. One of them read her diary and discovered she was a "snitch." The gang assigned three boys, all close friends of Brenda, to murder her. They took her on a fishing trip, then stabbed her to death. Brenda was pregnant at the time.

Leaving a gang can be difficult, especially if it is the only life an individual knows. However, it is not impossible. These are some of the reasons members choose to leave:

- *Aging*: Some lose the interest and energy they once had.
- *New activities*: New jobs, hobbies, and sports can shift their focus away from gangs.
- *Failed expectations*: Some feel they are not getting enough acceptance, appreciation, or action from their gang.
- *Violence*: After experiencing a violent lifestyle, members may become scared of harming or being harmed by others, of dying, or of getting arrested. If they get injured, they may begin to understand how their victims felt and change their attitudes.
- *Prison*: While it does not work for everyone, some young people who go to prison may reflect on their behavior and decide to change.
- *An improved family situation*: If people have joined a gang because of family issues, they may decide to leave if that situation improves.
- *Religion*: Those who join a religious group may embrace a new community of people and a new set of morals.

Leaving a gang

These are some of the ways that gang members have successfully left gangs and moved on with their lives:

- *Moving*: Sylvia Nunn, the Bloods' most ruthless female member, moved from Los Angeles to Las Vegas when her father became sick. There, she fell in love with a former sheriff, who made her choose between him and her gang lifestyle. She chose him.

Many police departments now offer **witness protection** programs for members who decide to leave gangs. The police help relocate these gang members to new areas, so that they can get a fresh start.

Although it is a painful process, some gang members choose to have their tattoos removed. This can help them start a new life.

- *Changing appearance*: One former member of the Crips says that he was often stopped by police or rival gang members if he left his territory. He began wearing neutral colors and styles. Now, he says, "I have the freedom to go anywhere." Changing appearance can be a powerful way to start a new life, but it should be done gradually. Any radical transformations might make gang members suspicious.

- *Anger management*: Former Gangster Disciple "Difficult" got out of her gang lifestyle by changing not only her appearance but also her attitude. She used to snap easily. Now she is more patient. Learning how to walk away from a fight or an insult is key to leaving a violent lifestyle.

- *Exit ceremonies*: To leave a gang, members sometimes have to endure another kind of ceremony, called a **Violation-out (V-out)** ceremony. Like a V-in, the member must endure a beating by other gang members. But the exit ceremony is often even more brutal, since gangs do not want their members to leave. They also want to remind members to never share any gang secrets with the outside world.

- *Buy-out*: In some gangs, members can buy their way out. Large, organized gangs often require hundreds of thousands of dollars in cash, but some smaller gangs will accept much smaller payments.

- *Walking away*: Butch Young joined the Crazy Homicides gang when he was 11. By the time he was 16, he had been arrested, dropped out of school, and seen his best friend stabbed. It was time to leave. Despite warnings of payback if he ever left, Butch simply stopped showing up at gang hangouts. No one ever came after him. Most teenagers do not get out as easily as Butch, but in general, the less involved a member is, the easier it is to leave.

- *Family matters*: Female gangsters who become pregnant are usually allowed and even encouraged to leave, to keep the unborn baby from danger. Some male gangsters who become fathers have gotten out, too.

It's not too late

If you are in a gang, it is not too late to get out. It is usually best to take small steps, starting with changes in appearance, friends, and activities. It is also important to find a supportive non-gang friend or mentor. Attending school is one of the best ways to avoid gang activity, while also preparing you for a brighter future.

Life after the gang

Some former gang members have managed to create successful lives for themselves.

WALTER'S STORY: FROM GANG TO GOVERNMENT

After Walter Burnett graduated from high school, he started hanging around with members of the Gangster Disciples gang in Chicago. One night, when he was 17, he and two older men drove to the town of Kankakee, Illinois, where they robbed a bank, stole a car, and kidnapped its driver. Walter pleaded guilty to armed robbery and served two years in prison. That was his wake-up call.

In prison, he spent time listening to motivational books and tapes and earning a two-year degree in mechanical drafting.

Once he got out, he got a degree in engineering and a job. He became involved in politics. He says he climbed his way up "by hard work and not being afraid to humble myself."

In 1995, he ran for alderman, an elected official representing a district of Chicago, and he won. In 2010, Chicago's police superintendent met with gang leaders from Chicago's West Side to discuss ways to reduce gang violence. He faced criticism for meeting with "criminals," but Alderman Burnett defended him, saying, "I'm happy. Gang leaders are calling me. They want to have a meeting. They want to talk about a truce in the community." They trust Burnett, because he once stood in their shoes.

SAROEUM'S STORY: MOLLY'S PROGRAM

When he was seven, Saroeum Phuong and his family escaped the brutal Khmer Rouge regime in Cambodia. After years in refugee camps, they settled in Boston, Massachusetts. That was when the real troubles started for Saroeum. His mother worked two jobs so the family could afford a house, but his father used all the money for gambling and alcohol. At school, Saroeum could not understand his teachers and was bullied.

Saroeum joined a Cambodian gang called the Boston Red Dragons. Since none of the members had money or jobs, they used guns to rob houses. Then Saroeum met Molly, who ran a street outreach program. At first he did not trust her, but she persisted. She would turn up on the street where he hung out with his friends. She convinced his school to let him stay when they wanted to kick him out.

However, Saroeum needed to get serious if he wanted to graduate. Since Saroeum could speak English better than he would write it, he asked his history teacher if he could learn about Cambodia and teach the other students. So, instead of hanging out, he began to read a lot. Saroeum graduated from high school and now works in Molly's program, helping other young people like himself. He says, "There's always a choice for people who are involved in a gang. Don't wait until it's too late."

The odds were against both Walter and Saroeum, but both managed to make successful lives for themselves. One thing they had in common was their willingness to take a look at their lives and admit they needed to make changes. Both of them also worked hard to finish school. This opened the door to opportunities they could never have imagined for themselves in their former lives as gang members.

ADVICE FROM CEASEFIRE

The CeaseFire Project started in Chicago and now operates throughout the United States and the world. It treats violence as a disease that can be prevented. The director of CeaseFire Illinois, Tio Hardiman, employs people called "violence interrupters" to help resolve conflicts before they erupt into violence. This group is featured in the movie *The Interrupters* (2011).

Here is what Hardiman has to say about gangs and violence:

Q: What are some of the biggest myths about gangs?

A: The biggest myth is that there are people making a lot of money out there. Another myth is that you need to be in a gang to have all the girls. You can just be a cool guy to get a girl. Another myth is that everyone out there is doing OK—because they've got these white T-shirts on and new gym shoes. But a lot of these people have nothing. They're just fronting (trying to appear better than they actually are).

Q: How can young people combat pressure they feel from peers to join a gang?

A: One way that a young person can combat peer pressure is to stay close to his own family, because those are the people that will be there for you in the end. Young people have got to stop trying to please other young people by showing how tough we are, because at the end of the day, when you turn 40 years old and you don't have a track record of working anywhere, and you don't have any degrees, and don't have any kind of history at all other than a violent history, you're going to find yourself being a **liability** to your family.

So, young people need to put more emphasis on their family and quit trying to uphold this whole code of the streets, because nobody wins. If you have **dysfunction** in your family, hopefully you'll have someone at school or a mentor that you can connect to—like in basketball, you have coaches that help with the fundamentals of understanding life. You've got to find a support system.

Q: If you could offer teenagers tips for dealing with gangs, what would they be?

A: Choose your friends carefully. And don't agree to something you really do not feel good about in your spirit. Make your own decisions—and if things have gone too far and you don't agree with something, detach yourself from the people involved, because whatever you don't stand up against is going to harm you one day. It's OK to walk away from a situation. This means that you are a thinking person—and you know what's best for your future.

Q: What can young people do to create better lives for themselves?

A: What I'd recommend is for kids to attach themselves to the most positive people they know. If you're in trouble, you need to say, "I'm in a bad situation, and I need some help." A lot of times a person's shame or guilt or their ego will not allow them to get the help they need. Life is a struggle for everybody. So, do not judge people, take your best shot at your life, and when all else fails, keep trying.

Steve James (third from the left) is the director of *The Interrupters*. He is with real-life "interrupters" (l to r) Cobe Williams, Ameena Matthews, Gary Slutkin, Tio Hardiman, and Eddie Bocanegra.

WHAT HAVE WE LEARNED?

Gangster movies, music, and video games can make the gang lifestyle seem thrilling. Gangsters may look like they have it all: girlfriends or boyfriends, money, and respect. However, underneath the gold chains, the white T-shirts, and the expensive shoes, many gang members have nothing at all.

Most gangsters have grown up in rough areas with poor schools and few positive role models. For some, a walk to the corner store is filled with danger. Many have buried friends or relatives killed in gang violence, and many come from broken homes or abusive families. For these young people, gangs may seem like the only way to find protection, acceptance, and respect.

However, gangs do not protect young people. Gangs keep them on the streets, away from classrooms and careers. Gangs send most of their members to prison or an early grave. Gang members kill other young people over things that, in the end, do not matter.

Marvin, 20, from Cape Town in South Africa, worked as a gang hit man. He turned his life around, thanks to a supportive family and a skills development academy for troubled young people.

Fortunately, even young people facing the most difficult circumstances can choose to walk away from a violent lifestyle. It may start with changing what they wear or who they hang out with. Or it may start with walking away from a fight or finding someone to help with homework. It could be as simple as asking an adult they admire what the next step should be.

Joining a gang has big consequences—for yourself and those around you. So, think about it. What do you really want your life to be like?

THINK ABOUT THIS

"Don't join gangs, because it's not worth it. When you reach my age (22), you'll have nothing to look back on or nothing to live off. If you're in a gang until my age, you won't have an education, you won't have money, and you won't have a job."
Kemar Harriott, ex-gang member

"All I can say to young people is: don't get caught up in the world of gangs. It's all lies. We fight to control territory that isn't ours to begin with. We cover ourselves with guns to show the world we are strong, but inside we are weak. As for me, by the time my eyes were opened, I was already in jail, paying with my life."
Alex Cisernos, former member of the MS-13 gang, spending life in prison for murdering his friend, gang member-turned-informant Brenda Paz, age 18

"My parents told me, if someone hurts me, to hurt them back two times more. So, I was always looking out for anybody who was trying to disrespect me, and then to get them back two times more was my plan. And that just led me into trouble, basically. I was 17 years old the first time I went to jail."
Gang member

RESEARCH AND DEBATE

You can find out more about gangs from a variety of sources. Think about whether your source is reliable and consider the perspective of the person who produced it. Might the person be trying to promote a particular point of view?

Books

Nonfiction books written for young people are an excellent source of accurate and accessible information. Written by professional writers and checked by experts, the materials have been designed especially for young readers and provide a balanced view of the topic, backed up by evidence. Check the publication date of the book and try to find the most up-to-date titles.

Web sites

Web sites run by respected, established organizations working to end gang violence are excellent sources of trustworthy information (see pages 54–55). They usually have case studies and quotes from people who have been in gangs, so you can find firsthand information about other people's experiences.

Firsthand information is also available from surveys about gangs. Organizations working with young people often publish the results of their research online. Check that the source is recent to ensure the information is up-to-date.

A warning about sources

Not all web sites are helpful or reliable. Anyone can set up a web site or blog and write what they like; no one checks if it is true or not. Beware of sites that are run by individuals and express their point of view alone.

Chat rooms on topics such as gangs can be a great way to interact with others who have shared similar experiences. Speaking with former gang members or gang prevention workers can help you feel supported and less alone. However, it is extremely important to use chat rooms with caution.

Since chat sessions are "live," users may say things that are inappropriate or even hurtful. Also, some young people you meet there might not even actually be young. They could be adults who want to hurt young people. Furthermore, gang members often use the Internet to recruit members, so make sure you never reveal personal information, such as your name or address, and never agree to meet anyone from a chat room in person.

Organize your research materials

If you are researching gangs for a school project, start by organizing your research materials into different categories. You could use the concept web below as a starting point:

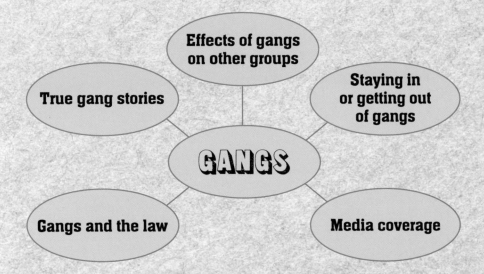

Using information for discussion and debate

If you are planning a discussion about gangs, remember that it is an extremely sensitive topic. There may be gang members in your school or people who have been their victims. It is important not to insult, anger, or upset anyone while discussing this topic. You may want to use role-playing in your debate. Different groups could adopt a different perspective on gang membership and argue from that point of view. You could also use the topics in the "Think about this" boxes in this book as discussion points.

GLOSSARY

abuse cruel or violent treatment of people

antisocial unwilling or unable to associate normally with other people; hostile or unfriendly toward others

assassination act of intentionally killing someone, usually a well-known public figure

bystander person who is present at an occurance without participating in it

card cloning converting a credit or debit card so that a customer's information and PIN are transferred wirelessly to an illegal third party

controversial something that produces debate or dispute between people on two different sides of an issue

domestic abuse pattern of behavior that causes physical or emotional harm to a partner in a relationship

drug trafficking buying, selling, or transporting illegal drugs

dysfunction not functioning normally; a breakdown of healthy relationships between members of a group

gang group of three or more people that participates in criminal or threatening activity within a community. Gangs usually have an identifiable name, symbol, territory, and code of conduct.

gangsta rap type of hip-hop music that depicts the violent lifestyles of inner-city young people, many of whom are gang members

graffiti images or lettering scratched, scrawled, painted, or marked in any manner on property

hip-hop style of music in which rhyming lyrics are chanted over a musical background

initiation rite admitting someone into a group by forcing him or her to overcome a challenge

intimidate frighten or threaten someone so that he or she does what you want

liability something that someone is responsible for

materialism tendency to value material possessions above everything else

negotiate work with another person or party to reach an agreement or resolution to a problem

notorious famous or well known, usually for a bad deed

peer person who is the same age and in the same social circle as you

post-traumatic stress disorder (PTSD) condition of mental and emotional stress occurring as a result of injury or severe psychological shock

semi-automatic gun that automatically reloads another bullet after each shot

sexted-in ritual that allows girls to join a gang by engaging in sexual activity with male gang members

sexual assault any sexual act in which a person is forced or persuaded (using threats) to engage in against his or her will, or any sexual touching of a person who has not agreed to it

skinhead often identifiable by having close-cropped hair and wearing heavy boots, skinheads are usually thought to be violent and racist

truce agreement to stop fighting

Violation-in (V-in) ceremony in which a potential gang member undergoes beatings at the hands of members of the gang he or she wishes to join

Violation-out (V-out) ceremony in which a gang member is given a brutal beating by fellow gang members in exchange for leaving the gang

white-collar crime non-violent crime such as identity theft

witness protection protection, usually by the police, for someone who has witnessed or reported a crime or informed police about unlawful activities. Some witnesses are given a new identity, moved away, and protected for the rest of their lives.

FIND OUT MORE

Books

Dudley, William, and Louise Gerdes, eds. *Gangs* (Opposing Viewpoints). Farmington Hills, Mich.: Greenhaven, 2005.

50 Cent. *From Pieces to Weight: Once Upon a Time in Southside Queens.* New York: Pocket, 2005.

Marcovitz, Hal. *Gangs* (Essential Issues). Edina, Minn.: ABDO, 2010.

Watkins, Christine, ed. *How Can Gang Violence Be Prevented?* (At Issue). Detroit: Greenhaven, 2007.

The following books contain some descriptions of gang life that may not be suitable for younger readers:
Sanchez, Reymundo. *My Bloody Life: The Making of a Latin King.* Chicago: Chicago Review Press, 2000.

Sanchez, Reymundo. *Once a King, Always a King: The Unmaking of a Latin King.* Chicago: Chicago Review Press, 2003.

Sanchez, Reymundo, and Sonia Rodriguez. *Lady Q: The Rise and Fall of a Latin Queen.* Chicago: Chicago Review Press, 2008.

Web sites

ceasefirechicago.org
Visit the web site of the CeaseFire Project to find out how this organization is working to prevent gang violence around the world.

gangsandkids.com
Intended for parents, this site also provides helpful statistics, links, and resources about gangs for teens, including the opportunity to read letters written by imprisoned former gang members.

www.ojjdp.gov/programs/antigang/
Learn what the U.S. government is doing to deal with gangs.

www.psn.gov
Project Safe Neighborhoods is a national organization that aims to end gun and gang violence in the United States. Visit its web site to learn about some of the outreach programs it organizes and more.

DVDs
Note: These DVDs contain some graphic footage of violence.

Crips and Bloods: Made in America (Docuramafilms, 2009)
This documentary explores the origins of the infamous Los Angeles street gangs known as the Crips and the Bloods.

Gangland (A&E Home Video, 2007–2011)
This History Channel series offers an inside look at some of the world's most notorious street gangs.

World's Most Dangerous Gang (Washington, D.C.: National Geographic, 2006)
This film offers a look at the fast rise of MS-13, one of the world's most brutal gangs.

Topics to debate
- What is the best method to stop violence? Is it best to reach out to the people most likely to engage in violence and show them new ways to resolve problems? Or are schools and employment opportunities in gang communities needed before violence can be stopped?
- Can gangs ever benefit a community? Some gangs require members to finish high school. Other give large donations to local clubs or sports teams to get the community on their side. Can these "benefits" ever outweigh increased violence and crime in the community?
- How do gang members today compare with the notorious gangsters of earlier times? Are they more or less dangerous? What are some things they have in common?

INDEX

alcohol and drug use 22, 31
anger management 43
antisocial 7

belonging, sense of 30

CeaseFire project 46–47, 55
code words 19
codes of conduct 16
colors 18, 43
commercial gangs 8, 9, 20, 31, 38
communication 6, 19
community "benefits" 27, 53
concept webs 51

deaths 5, 11, 17, 18, 22, 23, 32, 39
delinquent gangs 8, 9
dress code 17
drug dealing 6, 8, 9, 10, 16, 20, 32, 37, 38

education, lack of 22, 27

families of gang members 22

gang members
  age range 6, 10
  backgrounds 13, 28, 30, 48
  life expectancy 30
  reasons for joining gangs 30–31
  recruitment 6
  young members 9, 16, 21, 26
gangs
  girls and 10–13, 15, 38, 39, 41, 43
  identity 16–19, 24, 25
  impact of 22
  leaders 6

leaving a gang 12, 40–45
myths about 27, 46
names 6, 10
numbers of 6, 10
reasons for forming 24–27
territories 6, 20–21, 27
types of 8
gangsta rap 34–35
girl gangs 10–13
graffiti 21
guns 5, 6, 11, 12, 21

hand signs 19
Hays Code 35

imprisonment 10, 11, 22, 23, 30, 38–39, 40, 44, 49
informants 12, 16, 41
initiation rites 14, 15
innocent victims 5, 6, 17, 18, 22, 27, 32
Internet research 54–55
intimidation 8, 29, 32, 37

knives 6, 11, 12, 21, 22

leaving a gang 40–45
loyalty 6, 16, 18, 30

media attention 32–35
movies about gangs 35

peer pressure 30, 46
police 9, 10, 34, 36–38, 39, 42
police raids 38
prison gangs 39
punishments 16

racial and ethnic gangs 8, 24, 25
racial discrimination 24, 25, 37

respect 15, 16, 17, 29, 48
rival gangs 8, 9, 16, 20, 21, 22, 27, 39
role models 27, 31, 35, 38

school dropouts 27
self-esteem 13
settling scores 9, 22, 27
sex 10, 12, 13
sexted-in 15
social or street gangs 8, 26, 39
street safety 38
suburban gangs 8, 28

tagger gangs 21
tattoos 18
technology, use of 6, 19
territories 6, 20–21, 27
truces 38, 44

vandalism 8, 9
video games 7
Violation-in (V-in) 14, 15
Violation-out (V-out) 43
violence 5, 6, 7, 8, 15, 22, 23, 27, 34, 37, 39, 40, 46

white-collar crimes 12, 17
witness protection 42